DISCARD

Defining
MOMENTS

Christopher
REEVE

Don't Lose Hope!

002000292864

by Sunita Apte

CONSULTANT
Thomas Leitch
University of Delaware

BEARPORT
PUBLISHING COMPANY, INC.

New York, New York

Credits
Cover, AP/Wide World Photos/Eric Draper; Title page, © Patrick Robert/CORBIS
SYGMA; 4, © Lynn Goldsmith/CORBIS; 5, © ZUMA Archive/ZUMA/Corbis;
6–7 (both), Ken Regan/Camera 5; 8–9 (both), Ken Regan/Camera 5; 10, Courtesy
Jesse Shereff; 11, Seeley G. Mudd Manuscript Library, Princeton University,
Princeton, NJ; 12, Jenna Soleo, Courtesy The Julliard School; 13, AP/Wide World
Photos/ Steve Sands; 14, Photofest, New York; 15, Ken Regan/Camera 5;
16–17 (both), © Warner Bros. Courtesy Everett Collection; 18, © Leo Hsu/CORBIS
SYGMA; 19, AP/Wide World Photos /Elliot D. Novak; 20, Sesame Street and
associated characters, trademarks and design elements are owned and licensed by
Sesame Workshop. © 2005 Sesame Workshop. All rights reserved; 21, Ken Regan/
Camera 5; 22, Ken Regan/Camera 5; 23, Ted Thai/Time Life Pictures/Getty
Images; 24, Todd Warshaw/AFP/Getty Images; 25, The New York Times Agency;
26, Evan Agostini/Getty Images; 27, Ken Regan/Camera 5.

Editorial development by Judy Nayer
Design by Fabia Wargin; Production by Luis Leon; Image Research by Jennifer Bright

Library of Congress Cataloging-in-Publication Data
Apte, Sunita.
  Christopher Reeve : don't lose hope! / by Sunita Apte.
    p. cm. — (Defining moments)
  Includes bibliographical references and index.
  ISBN-13: 978-1-59716-074-2 (library binding)
  ISBN-10: 1-59716-074-1 (library binding)
  ISBN-13: 978-1-59716-111-4 (pbk.)
  ISBN-10: 1-59716-111-X (pbk.)
  1. Reeve, Christopher, 1952—Juvenile literature. 2. Actors—United States—
Biography—Juvenile literature. 3. Quadriplegics—United States—Biography—
Juvenile literature. I. Title. II. Series: Defining moments (New York, N.Y.)

PN2287.R292A88 2006
791.43'028'092—dc22

                                2005005222

For more information, write to Bearport Publishing Company, Inc.,
101 Fifth Avenue, Suite 6R, New York, New York 10003.
Printed in the United States of America.

10 9 8 7 6 5 4 3

Table of Contents

I Can't Move!

Christopher Reeve woke up. He was in a hospital bed. Around him were the worried faces of doctors and nurses.

Chris with his children, Matthew and Alexandra, before the accident

Chris at a horseback riding event days before his accident

More than 10,000 people are **paralyzed** in the United States each year.

What was he doing here? He didn't know. He tried to ask someone, but no words came out. Then he tried to sit up, but he couldn't move. In fact, he couldn't feel most of his body, including his arms and legs. What was going on?

Then someone told him the terrible news. Chris had been in a horse-jumping **competition**. He had fallen off his horse and broken his neck. Now he was paralyzed.

"You're Still You."

The news left Chris in shock. How could he live if he were paralyzed? He wouldn't be able to do anything. He would be a **burden** to his family.

Chris with his family after the accident

With an injury like Chris's, it can take weeks, months, or even years before the full damage is known.

Chris's wife, Dana, is an actor and a singer.

Chris decided he wanted to die. There was no reason to go on. Then someone changed his mind. It was his wife, Dana. She knew what Chris was thinking. She also knew that she would stand by him no matter what. Dana looked Chris in the eye and said, "You're still you. And I love you."

Those words saved Chris's life. He decided he wanted to live. He would find a way.

Learning to Live Again

Chris's life was going to be very different. He would have to learn how to live as a quadriplegic. A quadriplegic is someone who is paralyzed from the shoulders down. Chris couldn't move his arms or legs. He couldn't even breathe without a special tube. He needed help eating his meals and getting dressed.

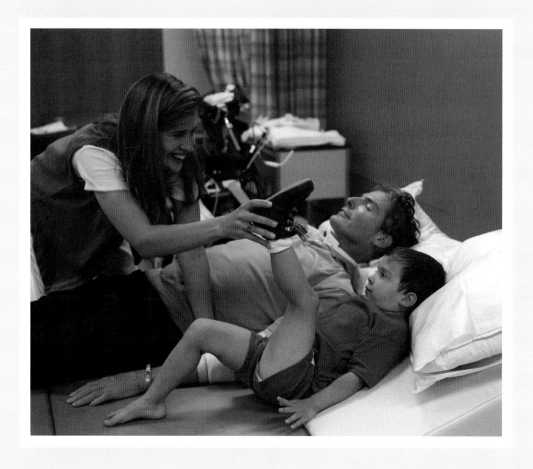

Chris gets some help with his physical therapy from Dana and their son, Will.

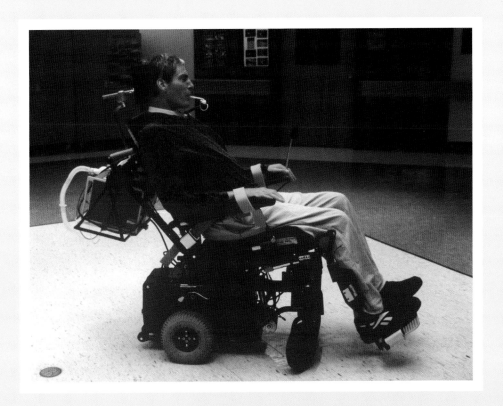

Learning to control a wheelchair with a straw can be harder than learning how to drive a car.

Chris had many new things to learn. For example, he couldn't roll his wheelchair with his arms. So he learned to move it by sipping and puffing on a special straw.

Chris's day began with "ranging." A nurse and aide slowly moved his arms and legs to keep them flexible.

Growing Up

Christopher Reeve was born in New York City. When he was four years old, his parents got divorced. He then moved to New Jersey with his mother and brother.

The divorce left Chris feeling sad and confused. He sometimes felt as if he had to choose between his parents.

The first **professional** show Chris appeared in was a musical called *The Yeomen of the Guard*. He was just nine years old.

When he was 18 years old, Chris (far left) appeared in the play Troilus and Cressida.

One day, when Chris was nine years old, members of a theater group came to his school. They were looking for kids to be in a play. Chris tried out and got a part. It changed his life forever.

Chris fell in love with acting. The theater was a place for him to escape from his **stressful** family life.

Becoming an Actor

Chris knew he wanted to be an actor when he grew up. However, his parents wanted him to go to college. Chris made a deal with them. He would go to college, but after he graduated he would pursue acting.

Chris attended drama classes at The Juilliard School in New York City.

There was only one other person in Chris's class at drama school. This student, named Robin Williams, went on to become a famous comedian and actor.

Chris's plan would have worked out if he hadn't been such a talented actor. At college, he was offered so many acting roles that it was hard for him to settle down and study.

With just one year of college left, Chris moved to New York City. He attended drama school while he finished college. He was ready to begin the life he had dreamed of.

"How Dare You Treat Your Mother That Way!"

One of Chris's first big roles was in the TV **soap opera** *Love of Life.* Chris played the character of Ben Harper. Ben was not a very nice guy. He didn't treat his friends or his family well.

The soap opera *Love of Life* ran on TV for 29 years!

Chris played Ben Harper on Love of Life *for two years.*

Chris spent some of the money he earned from acting on getting his pilot's license.

The soap opera had millions of fans, and many of them didn't think too highly of Ben's behavior. Once, at a highway rest stop, a woman came over to Chris and smacked him with her purse. "How dare you treat your mother that way!" she screamed. The woman didn't realize that Ben Harper was only a character that Chris was playing.

An Important Decision

Chris was getting more work as an actor, but he still wasn't a big star. Then, in 1977, Chris got a chance to **audition** for the leading role in the movie *Superman*.

At first, Chris didn't want to audition. He didn't think a serious actor should play a comic book character. Then he read the script and changed his mind. Chris went to the audition.

Chris did many of his own stunts in the movie, including hanging from wires during flying scenes.

To prepare for the role of Superman, Chris worked out and ate four meals a day, gaining 40 pounds (18 kg).

When the movie Superman came out, it earned more money in one week than any previous film.

That decision changed his life. Chris impressed the producers and got the part. *Superman* was a big hit. Chris became a rich and famous **international** movie star.

A Terrible Accident

Chris made three more Superman movies. After that, however, his career ran into trouble. Few people wanted to **cast** Chris as anyone but Superman.

Chris still acted in some plays and movies, but none of them were big hits. In his spare time, he played the sports he loved.

Chris loved horse jumping.
Here he is with his horse, Buck.

Chris makes a jump about two weeks before his accident.

The day Chris had his accident, he told a reporter, "Horse jumping is the most dangerous thing I do."

On May 27, 1995, Chris was in Virginia for a horse-jumping competition. The event began in the usual way, but then something went terribly wrong. While jumping over a fence, Chris's horse, Buck, suddenly stopped. Chris went sailing over Buck and landed on his head. His neck snapped, and he couldn't breathe. Chris was close to death.

Life Goes On

The **paramedics** and doctors managed to save Chris's life. He wasn't sure it was a life worth living, though, until Dana's words changed his mind.

Once Chris chose to live, however, he wanted to keep doing the things he loved. He appeared on TV, starred in a movie, and even directed a film. He also wrote an **autobiography** about his experiences.

Chris was a guest on Sesame Street, where he talked about life in a wheelchair.

Though paralyzed, Chris managed to stay active in the profession he loved. Here he is during the filming of the movie Rear Window.

Most of all, though, Chris wanted to walk again. Even though doctors told him it wasn't possible, he never gave up hope. He worked hard to exercise his body and stay in shape.

Chris won a Grammy Award for the spoken word version of his autobiography, *Still Me.*

It Moved!

In November 2000, five years after the accident, Chris and Dana were having a conversation at home. Suddenly, they noticed that Chris's index finger moved. They couldn't believe it. "Do that again," said Dana.

Chris used physical therapy equipment to stay as physically fit as possible.

Chris tried. "Move!" he said. His finger tapped against the chair. "Stop!" Chris commanded. His finger stopped. Chris and Dana were stunned. It turned out, however, that the finger was just the beginning. Soon, Chris could wiggle his toes, and straighten his arms and legs. He could sit up on his own, and he could even tell when someone was touching him.

A tilt table helps Chris practice standing.

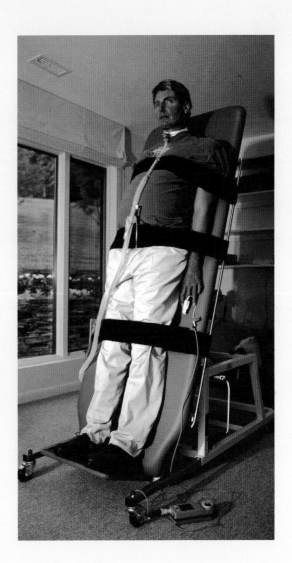

Most doctors didn't think it was possible to make such amazing progress after an injury like Chris's. He proved them wrong! Chris regained feeling on over 60 percent of his body.

The End Comes Too Soon

The world was excited by Chris's progress. Paralyzed people everywhere were given hope that they might walk again one day. People began talking about a cure for paralysis.

In December 2001, Chris carried the Olympic Torch.

Chris, too, was excited. He worked hard and made even more progress. His future looked bright. Unfortunately, events took a **tragic** turn.

A quadriplegic's health is always fragile. Someone paralyzed below the neck needs constant care and attention. Even then, things can go wrong. Sometimes they are **fatal.** On October 10, 2004, Christopher Reeve died from **complications** related to his injury.

From the time of his accident until he died, Chris had people helping him around the clock.

Christopher Reeve, 52, Symbol of Courage, Dies

By DOUGLAS MARTIN

Christopher Reeve, the cinematic Superman who became a real-life inspiration through his painstaking efforts to overcome total paralysis, while speaking out for stem-cell research and other potential treatments, died on Sunday at Northern Westchester Hospital in Mount Kisco, N.Y. He was 52 and lived in Pound Ridge, N.Y.

Mr. Reeve was being treated for a pressure wound, a common complication for people in wheelchairs, said his publicity agent, Wesley Combs. These wounds result from constant pressure in one spot, reducing the blood to that area and finally killing the affected tissue.

Mr. Combs said that Mr. Reeve fell into a coma on Saturday. The wound had become severely infected, and the infection spread through his body.

A riding accident in 1995 left the actor paralyzed from the neck down. After briefly pondering suicide, Mr. Reeve had become a powerful proponent of causes ranging from insurance reform for catastrophic injuries to unleashing the possibilities some scientists believe lie in using embryonic stem cells for research.

As recently as Friday, Mr. Reeve's name emerged, as it often has, in the national debate over stem cell use. In the presidential debate in St. Louis between President Bush and Senator John F. Kerry, the Democratic challenger, Mr. Kerry mentioned Mr. Reeve by name in arguing against the president's position that stem-cell research must be restricted to protect the lives of human embryos.

Yesterday, the White House issued a statement on behalf of the president and Mrs. Bush, citing Mr. Reeve as "an example of personal courage, optimism and self-determination."

As a young unknown actor Mr. Reeve propelled himself to the status of instant myth by starring in "Su-

Continued

Chris's death was a big story in newspapers, such as The New York Times, all over the world.

"Don't Give Up. Don't Lose Hope."

After the accident, Chris's life changed forever. Most people deal with terrible tragedies in private. However, as a well-known actor, Chris's tragedy was always in the public eye. He was able to use his fame to make people aware of what he and others faced each day. He fought endlessly to make things better for **disabled** people everywhere.

After his accident, Chris became a real-life superhero to millions of people.

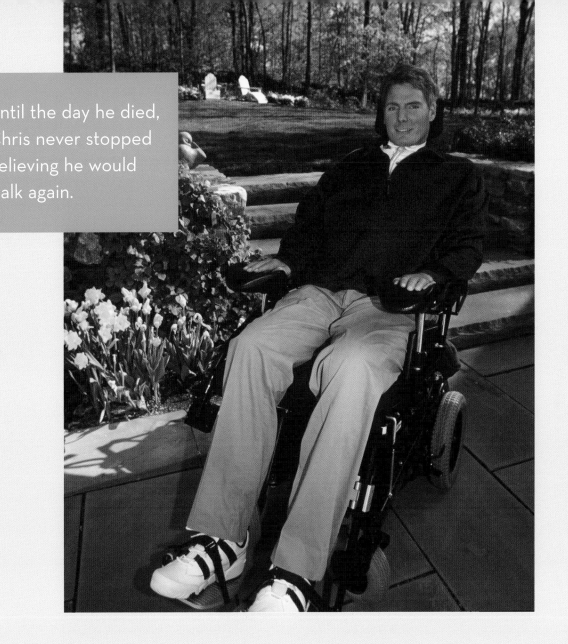

Until the day he died, Chris never stopped believing he would walk again.

Most of all, though, Chris showed people how to look toward the future with hope, even in their darkest hour. He helped people realize that true courage is making the best of life, no matter what happens. As Chris said, "Don't give up. Don't lose hope."

He never did.

Just the Facts

■ After Chris's parents got divorced, they both married again. So Chris grew up with a stepmother and a stepfather. He also became one of eleven children in his family.

■ In 1987, Chris traveled to South America to help save the lives of 77 actors in Chile. These people had been threatened with death by the man who ruled the country.

Timeline

Here are some important events in Christopher Reeve's life.

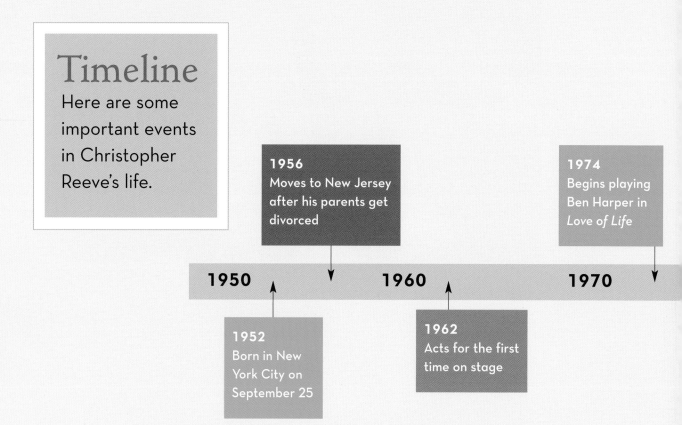

1956
Moves to New Jersey after his parents get divorced

1974
Begins playing Ben Harper in *Love of Life*

1950

1960

1970

1952
Born in New York City on September 25

1962
Acts for the first time on stage

■ After his accident, Chris had to make changes to his home to meet his medical needs. He added an entire wing, widened doorways, and replaced stairs with ramps.

■ Chris created his own foundation for paralyzed people in 1996. The Christopher Reeve Paralysis Foundation raises money to help find a cure for paralysis. The foundation also works to improve the quality of life for people who are paralyzed.

■ Chris spent a lot of time working with members of Congress to push for laws that would help disabled people. He even addressed a session of Congress on the subject.

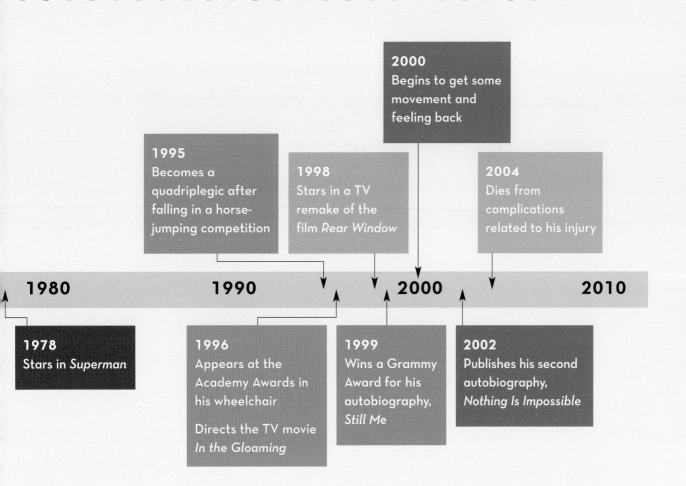

2000
Begins to get some movement and feeling back

1995
Becomes a quadriplegic after falling in a horse-jumping competition

1998
Stars in a TV remake of the film *Rear Window*

2004
Dies from complications related to his injury

1980   **1990**   **2000**   **2010**

1978
Stars in *Superman*

1996
Appears at the Academy Awards in his wheelchair

Directs the TV movie *In the Gloaming*

1999
Wins a Grammy Award for his autobiography, *Still Me*

2002
Publishes his second autobiography, *Nothing Is Impossible*

Glossary

audition (aw-DISH-uhn) the act of trying out for a play, movie, or concert by performing something in front of judges

autobiography (*aw*-toh-bye-OG-ruh-fee) a book about a person's life, written by that person

burden (BUR-duhn) a heavy responsibility that weighs someone down

cast (KAST) to choose who will perform in a movie or play

competition (*kom*-puh-TISH-uhn) contest

complications (*kom*-pli-KAY-shuhns) problems caused by an illness or injury that are related to, but not part of, the illness or injury

disabled (diss-AY-buhld) unable to do certain things because of an illness or injury

fatal (FAY-tuhl) resulting in death

international (*in*-tur-NASH-uh-nuhl) known by people all over the world

paralyzed (PA-ruh-lized) unable to move parts of one's body

paramedics (*pa*-ruh-MED-iks) people who ride in ambulances and give life-saving first aid

professional (pruh-FESH-uh-nuhl) making money for doing something

soap opera (SOHP OP-ur-uh) a daytime TV series containing characters with exciting and sometimes unrealistic lives

stressful (STRESS-fuhl) making someone feel anxious or tense

tragic (TRAJ-ik) very sad or unfortunate

Bibliography

Reeve, Christopher. *Nothing Is Impossible.* New York: Random House (2002).

Reeve, Christopher. *Still Me.* New York: Random House (1998).

Slater, Eric. "'Superman' Star Christopher Reeve Dies." *Los Angeles Times,* October 11, 2004.

Wren, Laura Lee. *Christopher Reeve: Hollywood's Man of Courage.* Berkeley Heights, NJ: Enslow (1999).

Read More

Abraham, Philip. *Christopher Reeve.* Danbury, CT: Children's Press (2002).

Alter, Judy. *Christopher Reeve: Triumph Over Tragedy.* Danbury, CT: Franklin Watts (2000).

Hughes, Libby. *Christopher Reeve (Taking Part).* Parsippany, NJ: Dillon Press (1997).

Kosek, Jane Kelly. *Learning About Courage from the Life of Christopher Reeve.* New York: PowerKids Press (1999).

Learn More Online

Visit these Web sites to learn more about Christopher Reeve:

www.christopherreeve.org/
www.usatoday.com/life/people/2004-10-11-reeve-obit_x.htm

Index

About the Author

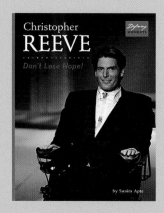

SUNITA APTE is a children's book author living in Brooklyn, New York. When she's not writing books for kids, she likes to cook and travel the world.